LOST AT SEA
POETRY, FICTION & MEMOIRS

Written and Edited by The Students of
EQUIPO ACADEMY

CODEX PUBLISHING, A DIVISION OF THE WRITER'S BLOCK, INC.
DOWNTOWN LAS VEGAS, NV

LOST AT SEA
POETRY, FICTION & MEMOIRS WRITTEN BY
THE STUDENTS OF EQUIPO ACADEMY

Over the course of the 2017 and 2018 school year, Corey Wozniak's tenth grade students at Equipo Academy developed the skills to eloquently express their ideas in poetry and prose. This book is a representation of those students' creative achievement. Making this book took hundreds of hours of combined effort in writing, reading, editing, and artistic direction, and the students' hard work has paid off. This collection of stories, memoirs, and poems truly reflects the diversity of thought and experience that make the students of Equipo Academy extraordinary.

EDITORIAL COMMITTEE
Elvis, Arias, Esmeralda Arroyo, Noah Baldridge, Marisol Diaz, Alondra Padilla, Andrea Padilla and Diego Padilla

CONTRIBUTING EDITORS
Frank Johnson, Scott Seeley and Corey Wozniak.

Copyright © 2018 by Equipo Academy, The Writer's Block, Inc. and the authors. All rights reserved. No part of this publication may be reproduced without the prior written permission of The Writer's Block Inc.

The Writer's Block and Codex and colophon are registered trademarks of The Writer's Block Inc.

www.equipoacademy.org   www.thewritersblock.org

Printed in Downtown Las Vegas, the United States of America.

Save this book for when you are older.

TABLE OF CONTENTS

Part One
THE BERMUDA TRIANGLE

Abraham Esqueda	*No MERCY*	11
Abraham Esqueda	*Dreams*	13
Emely Alarcon	*The Begging*	15
Marisol Diaz	*Butterfly Effect*	17
Noah Baldridge	*Daddy Issues*	19
Kylie Cazares	*My Voodoo Doll*	21
Marizela Montalvo	*My Favorite Love Story*	23
Jaquelyn Martinez	*A Different Life*	27
Jaquelyn Martinez	*Illegal Freedom*	29
Arturo Barraza Soto	*Young Mexican*	31
Miguel A. Oliva	*Is Life Fair?*	33
Alejandro Renteria	*Bentley 2056: A Sci-Fi Story*	35

Part Two
WHALE OF A TIME

David Henry	*Fan Fiction: Hunger Games*	39
Jacob Sellers	*Sin City*	40
Diego Padilla	*The Duel*	41
Angel Obeso-Ferracin	*Las Vegas*	43

Noah Baldridge	*Book Covers*	44
Leo Benitez	*DECISIONS*	45
Abraham Esqueda	*Getting to Know My Father*	47
Andrea Padilla	*Magic*	51
Marisol Diaz	*Sew Your Love into Me*	55
Marisol Diaz	*Through the Eyes of a Mother*	61
Abraham Esqueda	*I'm Not Sorry*	63
Kylie Cazares	*My Mom's Perfume*	65

Part Three
ANCHORS

Bryan Herrera	*This I Believe...*	
	About the Afterlife	69
Carlos Lainez	*The Truth*	71
Marisol Diaz	*The Wandering Girl*	73
Emely Alarcon	*This One's For You*	77
Elvis Arias	*Explaining My Happiness*	
	to My Mom	81
Angel Obeso-Ferracin	*Leonardo DaVinci*	82
Marizela Montalvo	*Change My Mind*	83
Jaquelyn Martinez	*Guadalupe*	85
Manuel M.	*El Moises Barragan: A Tribute*	87
Angel Obeso-Ferracin	*He Can't Say Goodbye*	89

Part Four
DEEP DARK WATER

Kevin Hernandez	*Dream of the Forest*	93
Marizela Montalvo	*Lovesick*	95
Emely Alarcon	*This One's for You*	97
Esmeralda Arroyo	*Hellevator*	101
Noah Baldridge	*Lemonade*	103
Noah Baldridge	*Utah*	105
Esmeralda Arroyo	*Nyx*	107
Jacob Sellers	*I'm Straight*	111
Kylie Cazares	*Baba Yaga*	113
Steve Arroyo	*New Cat in the Hood*	117

Part Five
HORIZONS

Alondra Padilla	*God's Ears are Never Open When I Speak*	121
Bibi	*Identity Essay*	123
Marisol Diaz	*Youngiae*	125
Kylie Cazares	*Rhyme Poem*	129
Angel Obeso-Ferracin	*El Principe*	131
Noah Baldridge	*Valentine*	133
Jaquelyn Martinez	*What My Parents Expected*	135
Jaquelyn Martinez	*Say It Before It's Too Late*	137
Nereida Delgado	*I Believe That People Should Not Be Homophobic*	139
Emely Alarcon	*The Curly Headed*	141
Kylie Cazares	*This I Believe... About Love*	145
Carlos Ordaz	*Sato and Veronica*	149
Author Biographies		151

Part One
THE BERMUDA TRIANGLE

No MERCY
By Abraham Esqueda

The term equalizer. To me it means being even and being the same. Just like in sports when you are down by one point and you score one so that was the equalizer. Although, to think about death being an equalizer. Let me tell you about payback. That ain't always the way to settle ways in real life. Let's just say that death is the great equalizer. Oh yes! Look I'm gonna kill this guy so that I can avenge my friend. No. The dude that killed your friend didn't really earn it. That was his problem, it was his idea, and his fault. Killing the guy wouldn't help. Now you would be just like him. Your friend who died wouldn't want that. To think that you avenged your friend is nice, but not death.

Death is the great equalizer. What does that mean!? Ok that is nice if you're playing a video game. Enemies are everywhere and we can't always fix that. We can't unite with these people and what really happened. We ignore the situation think about tell it ruins our lives and do something bad. We avenge our friend, but we create a new problem. I believe that is not the answer and that there is more options in doing when you want to equalize or something. Death is not no type of equalizer. So why even think about it that way. I know that if my friend was shot and killed he would like to be remembered. Remembered as the good guy that he was not to be avenged somehow and bring that bad out of his friend which is me. It's not right to take another man's life for another man's life. It just doesn't add up. That would just be a loophole. If there was many killings for avenging and death being the equalizer. Then it won't stop until there is no one else to kill. Besides that there is no going around that or thinking of a different way to describe this statement.

So which is why I chose to disagree because I believe that causing a death to make things equal or even is false. Many ways I can explain this sentence of death being the equalizer. Although I know that if you put it into thought you know what I mean. Put in a situation like that and you won't have the guts to become the equalizer. You won't have the guts to think of punishing someone with death, well maybe think about it but not take action. You never know till you know, you know?

DREAMS
By Abraham Esqueda

Yo I don't know if it's me or the Universe
But I think my dreams feel like a different life
and when I wake I'm cursed
Imagine you living all well
then you open a new door to hell
Nope that wouldn't happen
because of when I threw that quarter in the well
Just gotta live life
and think of every time that you made yourself pride
You know that your mission is just to live life

The Begging
By: Emely Alarcon

You got me hooked
Hooked like a book that has that first juicy line
Like she has the knife in her had full of blood and she doesn't
Know what to do.
You where that first line for me and just
like that i was stuck on you

Every love lyric in song reminded me of you
Your name would pop up in my head like
Melody I could never forget.
Just the hum of your name brought all
The memories flowing inside my head.

I remember the first time we exchange words
That simple hello that made my face turn red.
Like if someone was choking me and I was
Trying to gasp for air.

You made me happy

You were my drug I would
Get high just be looking at you.
You were addictive like every touch from you
Pink luscious lips would drag me in further,
Further in the black hole of your love.

Your face stuck with me forever
I could remember those eye that stood
At from mile away. I could recognize your hands
It had rough exterior like sandpaper.
And your soft, silky, hair, that you would always
Complain about going in your face,
I loved all of you and i still do.

Your lips were covered with a love potion
So sweet, It tasted like gold covered in layers of sugar
Glazed with honey. Leaving me to want more
You had me under your spell, wrapped around
Your fingers.

I could hear my heartbeat get louder and louder
Like the beats from a drum. You made my heart
Want to burst out of my chest and explain the
Feelings I have for you, because the
words wouldn't come out my mouth.
I was speechless when it came to you

I Love you

The Butterfly Effect
By Marisol Diaz Nunez

A reality that seems like a dream,
the foggy look on your face
It doesn't convince me, please don't disappear on me
I'm scared that if I let go you will fly away,
and break away from my reality.
Like a butterfly, that once appeared in my dreams
That left me wondering if you were really here
Your light shines bright through this darkness
that is the butterfly effect

Daddy Issues
By Noah Baldridge

Something all too common.
Like cancer nowadays.
Eating away slowly at your health,
Like when he refused to pay child support,
Slowly at your finances, like when he stole me
and my brother's Christmas money.
Churning away in the pit of my being
like voices in my head,
Constantly saying "He didn't want you".
Whispering "He has his own family now,
you're just a failed attempt".
Its like amputation, gone forever
but always a phantom pain.
My mental state is like a animal carcass,
He's the vulture pecking away at me,
Feeding off my pain
A constant emptiness, in me, my home,
the table set for dinner.
Its like i was set up,
he was there just long enough for me
to get attached and ripped a like a scab,
And from that i was bled dry.
But I came back stronger,
you think I'd just go down crying for daddy?
Fuck no.
I can't tell you how many times he's tried to come back.

I let him once, and you know what he did?
"Forgot" my clothes at his house and "forgot"
to not sell them for drug money.
Remember the saying "No man left behind"?
Well, I got left behind,
Along with a brother and a single mom
fending for herself in a world of wolves,
While he's fresh out of rehab with his 4 kids and wife
that all adore their clean daddy.

My Voodoo Doll
By Kylie Cazares

My voodoo doll
You see darkness with a small lit candle
Valuable is what i would like to call it
On one hand it's the broken heart
On the other hand it could be a needle
Don't judge my doll for the way it looks,
you don't sense the sweetness like I do.
Offer her a gift of love
Offer her a hand for friendship
Don't look into its eyes or you'll love it as much as i do
On the day you fall in love
Life will be different
Life will never let you be alone or empty
Hope is what she'll give you
Everything will be okay,
never will she stab you in the back
Life will be a lot better when you know her
People believe she's their light
Maybe she'll love you just as much
Even if you hold her heart and needle

My Favorite Love Story
By Marizela Montalvo

Of course he wasn't going to approach her, she already had kids. Who'd want to raise 6 other kids at such a young age? Felix Herrera, was 22 years old when he first saw Socorro Carrera at 16 years of age, who then became the love of his life. " Nunca me imaginaba estar con esa hermosa muchacha que vi en el parque esa tarde," he states.

One boring afternoon in La Candela, Durango, Mexico, Felix decided to accompany his little cousin to the only "fun" place there, the park. After 15-20 minutes of being there, he spotted Socorro. Right below her, he then saw little kids all around her. He's extremely shy and didn't want to go up to her and strike up a conversation. Instead, he asked one of his older cousins about her since everyone in the little town knows each other. He asked her if those were her kids and who her parents were. Turned out that he had worked for them before and so he knew them. His cousin then told him that her family was huge, she had 13 siblings and she would take care of some of them. After knowing that, he approached her. But, before he did my grandma had already had an eye on him. She said he looked really reserved and "manly." After that day they kept talking and would meet up at the park to hang out. My grandma took him home so that he could meet her parents because they would ask why she would always want to go to the park so much and she told them the truth, that it was because of a guy. My great grandparents were extremely strict but they really liked him, they thought he was a good guy for her but they were kinda scared because he was older. At the same time they liked the fact that he was because that meant that he was mature and wasn't just there to play with their "little girl's" heart and he was going to take good care of her and protect her. They lectured him and told him that if he wanted to be with her, he had to follow certain rules—and so he did.

      A month later, my grandpa told her terrible news: he was going to have to move to Chicago because his family had found him a job out there that would pay him well. Of course, he couldn't miss out on that amazing opportunity, so he packed his bags and left to take advantage of the opening! My grandma was heartbroken and felt very lonely since she had gotten used to hanging out with him almost every afternoon at the park that they had met at. While he was in Chicago they wrote to each other because that was the only way that they were able to communicate. They wrote letters back and forth for a whole year! Then, he returned back to Mexico and the day he got there he asked her to be his girlfriend! Two weeks later, they got married by the church and threw a party. My grandma said that she had a lot of fun at her wedding but a few things didn't go as planned. First, the photographer that they were supposed to have lagged on them because he got sick. Also, after their church ceremony, they were supposed to walk to the banquet followed by a band and their guests. (Everything in the town is walking distance.) As the church started coming to an end, a storm began so everyone had to get a ride there. After the wedding which ended at 5am , they did a traditional after party, which is to go to the bride's house and eat again. I asked " que comieron?" Socorros' face lit up and flashed a big smile and said " Mi papa me mato una vaca y la cocinamos toda, no quedo nada!"

After 2 months of living in Durango, Mexico they decided to come to the United States and find a "better" life here. Two months after living in Los Angeles, California my grandma found out that she was going to be a mom for the first time! " Ni estaba nerviosa, ni triste nada malo! Estaba bien contenta porque ya tenía experiencia y queria un baby! Estabamos bien contentos los dos!" Socorro exclaimed. Felix then said "Si, estabamos muy felices. Bueno yo queria un niño pero luego nos dimos cuenta que iva ser una niña y pues es tu mama! Estábamos bien contenta con ella y estaba bien chula y chiquita tambien. Luego nuestro segundo baby era un nini, tu tio. Los queríamos mucho, y siempre sera asi," he said with his voice cracking, almost about to cry.

What really warmed my heart during this interview, was when i asked my grandpa about how the wedding went he stated " Me siento muy agusto contando esta historia después de tantos años que han pasado y que cuando tengamos 50 años de casados espero que Marizela nos haga la boda de oro. También quiero tener el honor de ver a Marizela casada asi de blanco como nos casamos nosotros." When he said that I literally shed a tear, it was so cute, my grandpa is my dad figure and that coming from him made me feel so good. " Boda de Oro " is another tradition that we have done for a while. It is pretty much another wedding celebrating their 50th anniversary.

I hope to have the love life my grandparents have one day. It's so pure and I love it so much! Theyre so positive, loving and supportive. Not only with themselves, but with everyone else. They never really argue or have any problems. My grandpa even said himself " hemos estado mucho mas felices que infelices" which is very true! I look up to them so much and I really hope they keep on supporting me and help me better myself everyday because i look up to them and love them so much. Wishing love and happiness to all relationships.

A Different Life
By: Jaquelyn Martinez

One morning I woke up in clothes that aren't mine and in a room that wasn't my room, and I thought to myself "what In the world did I do last night". While I tried to remember my night I shuffled around the room looking for my things, but after what seemed like an eternity of looking I gave up and went for the door. Cracking the door open just enough to peek my head through and make sure no one was around, I tiptoed out of the room and carefully closed the door behind me. I started sneaking around the house, like a ninja, trying to find a way out. Just then i found the kitchen and a door that lead outside,just as I was about to dash to the door some short, thin, lady quickly stepped in front of me and said "mija I made you pancakes". I must've looked puzzled because she chuckled and told me to sit. So I walked as casual as possible and plopped into one of the chairs. "This must be some sort of mistake, this isn't my home and you aren't my mom". The lady walks over with a plate of pancakes in her hand "Are you practicing for acting class or something Amanda?" "No, I'm being serious ma'am this isn't my home." The lady looked at me confused, "Mija, we've lived here for the past sixteen years." I sat there baffled, trying to think of last night once again but nothing seemed to come to mind. "Huh, I don't seem to remember anything from last night". This lady, who says is my mother, smiles " of course you don't silly, you fell asleep on the couch around

5." I sat there trying to process everything, "Are you saying that I dreamt a whole different life in my sleep and don't remember my real life?". "I'm guessing, now c'mon sweetie you're going to miss the bus, we'll talk after school."

Illegal Freedom
By Jaquelyn Martinez

I am an illegal immigrant
And I refuse to believe that
I can live my life freely
I realize this may be a shock, but
"THe streets are made of gold"
Is a lie
"Everybody is not treated equally"
In 30 years, I will tell my children that
I have my priorities straight because
Fear
Is more important than
Living
I tell you this:
Once upon a time:
I was given the chance to be free
But this will not be true in my era
I will live caged, in my fears
Experts tell me
I will be deported
I do not conclude that
I will live in peace without being hunted
In the future,
I will be in my hometown that I know nothing of
NO longer can it be said that
I will be in the states getting a better future
It will be evident that

I will be judged
It is foolish to presume that
I will make it in this country
And all of this will come true unless we reverse it.

Young Mexican
By Arturo Barraza Soto

Me being middle class and mexican is what really made me who I am. The way it made me like this was because I was not really able to do what other kids did. when I came here people treated me like a criminal and because I wasn't able to afford nothin much. One time when I was stopped for jaywalking a cop slammed me to the car but I really didn't do anything to make him slam me. Those two things made me humble because I didn't treat people different me. One thing that made me accept me who I really am is when I got expelled for the first time I was just thinking if I really am a criminal but when I had a conference with the teachers at my old school they had told me I wasn't a bad kid that I didn't have to turn out like other kids who wanna act like other people. Than I thought to myself that just because i'm middle class undocumented mexican doesn't mean I have to act criminal like people say. So I think my identity is being a chill humble undocumented mexican even though i'm being targeted I don't really care because my vibe is to be chill. My identity is different from lots others.

Is Life Fair?
By Miguel A. Oliva

I believe life is fair. Sometimes in life, everything can be going great or seem perfect, but as soon as you know it karma can catch up with you, or a bitch called life can punch you right in the gut without any warning.

One day as I was hanging out with my friends having a good day at school. I come home to hear the news that my grandma just passed away. I was shocked. When I said bye 3 months ago I was sure that wasn't the last time. I should've appreciated the time I spent with her more. If I knew I would've...

What about a special person that you deeply cared about intimately? You know, that person that gives you butterflies every time you see them, and has your tongue all twisted and turned when you talk to them, and your heart starts racing. Have you ever felt that feeling being destroyed? Like it was put in a blender and juiced right in front of you without you being able to do anything. It feels like that spot where your heart was is now empty.

Later that week I woke to experience that feeling, that special person was gone. What a great start to the weekend. My head filled with an influx of questions as I got dressed for school. What did I do? What happened? Why? I didn't know how to react. That didn't feel good at all.

That weekend I was starting to have premonitions of bad things, but I tried to look at the bright side, I guess it could've been worse. But is that all that happens in life, bad things? But then I thought back to something Johnny Depp once said, " Breath, it's only a bad day, not a bad life". That was true, the good things life had to offer me are in the future, but I had kept in mind that bad things would intervene too.

The next week I felt great for some odd reason. I woke up to find out my baby cousin was born! I couldn't wait to see him and play around with him. I arrived at school and they handed out quarter 4 report cards during class, I had all B's. I was excited because I knew that was going to make my mom happy. As the week passed by summer arrived, school was finally over. It seemed like I waited forever. My cousins came into town, we had a blast doing dumb stuff and in trouble but nothing too deep. Within that summer break, I got to travel to New Mexico and visit my cousin that had just been born and the rest of my family. We had cookouts and barbecues every day and I got to hang out with my other cousins. I even started talking to an old friend again that helped me get through tough times.

That summer was great, I learned that no matter what happens in life, it'll get better. You just have to learn to not let it phase you and keep your head up high no matter what because life is life, it can be shitty sometimes. Sunny days wouldn't be special if it wasn't for rain, and Joy wouldn't feel good if it wasn't for pain. Besides, Who said life was easy?

Bentley2056: A Sci-Fi Story
By Alejandro Renteria

Although, I always wished to buy myself the new self driving Bentley even though my family thought it was not a good idea. "C'mon Woody you never know if that thing ever gets hacked and maybe even kills you" his older brother Buzz quoted with a very anxious voice while shrugging his shoulders.

"Right woody imagine one day out of nowhere it grows some giant robotic legs and turns on the whole city" said Rex insisting that Woody would not buy the new Bentley.

"Ahh y'all just talking nonsense that'll never happened, the car may drive itself but I doubt it'll ever become that dangerous" claimed woody.

"We just think it's not a good idea to invest money on an expensive ass car when you could buy a cheaper car and actually drive it yourself, that's why cars were invented right?" Questioned Buzz

"Yes but imagine just being laid back playing fortnite on your phone while your car drives you to your destination by itself, that would be amazing!" Excitingly said woody with a giant smile on his face like if he had seen a huge pile of donuts.

"That does sound awesome, well of course your decisions are your decisions don't say we did not try to stop you" said Rex with a very shaky voice.

About 5 days after Woody bought his murdered out, with 22' billets Bentley, he decided to visit his girlfriend Jessie, he noticed that his check engine light was on so he pulls over to the nearest gas station. He pops the hood and then hops out to check the engine and notices that nothing's wrong with his car. So he gets back on and re-enters his girlfriends address. While on his way his car anonymously grew some gigantic steel arms and legs. The computer inside randomly starts talking to Woody saying stuff like " You dirty humans have been killing earth for the past 50,000 years now it's time for us to take care of business!" As soon as the computer says that it start smashing everything in its way and everything around it. Keep in mind woody is struggling to get out of the gigantic monster but the doors are jammed. From a distance you can see a lot of other self driving cars turn into humongous robots and every single one of them destroying anything it sees. The city had turned into chaos. Woody has no idea how to stop it and is struggling to get out of the car when the computer surprisingly starts talking again but this time it says something different! "Self destructing in 5… 4… 3… 2… 1…"

(KABOOOM)

Part Two
WHALE OF A TIME

Fan Fiction: Hunger Games
By David Henry

Katniss and Peeta are running for their lives from a group of rival competitors. "When we catch you, we're going to use your bones as weapons!" shouted one of them. Katniss and Peeta have run out of weapons and are starving. "They're gaining on us!" yelled Peeta in a shaking voice. Katniss turned around to get a glimpse of the rival competitors. Bang! Katniss ran into a tree and was knocked out cold. Peeta shouthed, "Katniss!" He turned around and began shaking her unconscious body. "We have to go!" Now less than six yards away the rival competitors began laughing at the helpless Katniss Everdeen and Peeta Mellark. Peeta stood up and yelled at the rival competitors who now only a couple feet away, "Please let us live!" The rival competitors laughed and began slashing at Peeta with swords. "Katniss! Wake up!" He yelled out in agony at Katniss' still unconscious body. "Lets kill her later, I want her to wake up and see his dead body." said one the rival competitors while pointing at Katniss. THey all agreed and walked away leaving Peetas dead body bleeding out next to Katniss. A couple hours left Katniss woke up to see Peetas dead mutilated body. She cried and hugged him getting blood all over her clothes. "Why? It's all my fault!" She cried out with a revengeful look on her face.

Sin City
By Jacob Sellers

I met this girl named Sindy
The day I came out my mother
She was well known
All across the world
She was hot as fuck but
There was so many people
Going in and out her
She looked like bright lights
Shining through a storm,
From the outside
But inside she's full of greed and lies
She pulls you in with all her beauty
Then takes your money
All in one night
You put a lot of money in her
But what you get in return
Isn't worth it

The Duel
By Diego Padilla

He was face to face with Ol' One-Eyed Willy, his arch enemy. His scabbed hands grabbed the holt of his silver revolver. His nostrils widened with deep breaths. His black hat was dusty. His finger wiggled hold of his revolver and says, "Any last words boi?"

Then he jerks his hand and scares Ol' One-Eyed Willy

"Ooh Wee Marston you got me there I'll tell u that but, you ain't faster den me tho," he says.

Ol' willy grasps his gun and cocks it back then BANG!! Ol` One-Eye Willy drops dead to his knees.

John chuckles, "Rookie mistake my friend rookie mistake... don't forget I'm the best sharpshooter there is in the west boi."

John loots the man's body and takes his valuables then turns to the ladys and says, "He won't be bothering you ladies anymore I can assure you that." The ladies tell him, "Thank you mister John Marston thanks for helpin us out."

John whistles for his horse and saddles up and says, "I'm a man of my word ladies," with a tilt in his hat and rides off into the sunset.

Las Vegas
By Angel Obeso-Ferracin

I met this guy
When I was 5 years old
And what I loved most
Was the money in his hands,
And stacks in his pockets.
112 years old, with green colored eyes like dollars
Stunning his money, looking 25.
Million dollar car,
Thousand dollar clothes.
Pulling in all the hoes,
Acting selfish.
Cali said pass some,
Vegas responded "You funny if you think you even getting one."
Getting older and older,
Richer and richer.

Book Covers
By Noah Baldridge

Family fun is on the run
Illegally being free
Is it legal to be me?
A good message faces constant prejudice
Looks judged like books
Framed as crooks and being booked.
It's unfair that the others are spared
But such is life,
Just like some ink makes you rethink if he safe
Or if as soon as you turn your back
your stomach will churn
Even if he's the good guy that not what the cover says
So take cover and let him burn
Judge the book by its cover and hide behind mother
Thats what its come to
Yet I still hope to come to
With a new world born a-new
The unorthodox should not make us jump out our socks.
Stay in school
Don't let the covers rule you
Be a lover
And especially,
Don't judge a book by its cover.

DECISIONS
By Leo Benitez

As a kid, I always believed that is you did something bad or good didn't matter. You always be recompensed of your deed. Let's say, for example, I gave money to a homeless person who needed; according to the law of recompense, sometime in the near future I would be repaid for my act of kindness. The opposite could also happen: if you did something very bad, something very bad would come back to you. Some people call this KARMA.

When I was around 8, I remember I would always go home after school do my work then go outside to play and this was the time around late December, early January, and I had gotten this really cool bike for christmas. I will never forget it. I remember that's all I asked for that whole year and I was super happy to wake up the next looking forward to just riding it all day and I could remember this one time I was heading home I was walking with my sister and there was a football just on the ground and I didn't see nobody come for it at all it just lied there and I picked it up and ended up taking it home with me and this is where I made a mistake I should have never took something that didn't belong to me. So then next couple of days pass, and I remember my mom calling me in because it was getting dark out and I was way too lazy to move my bike inside so I left it outside for the night and I could remember waking up the next day supper happy waiting to ride my bike and when I walked out of the door I could tell immediately that mike bike had been stolen and as a little kid I was crying for a week straight I could remember telling everyone at school if they've seen my red bike anywhere and I didn't get nothing at the end of the day

    MORAL of this story is never take something that's doesn't rightfully belong to you because as you can see karma's gonna end up coming for you whether it is bad or good.

Getting to Know My Father: A Personal Essay
By Abraham Esqueda

Many non-intimidating goofy groups of Mexican teenagers surrounded the center of the carnival. Throughout their groups there was the cockiness the was flowing through their groups. To hype each other up they grooved with the music that played in the background of the carnival. Juan Esqueda, oh what a cocky little sun of a gun that this kid was. He was within a group of Mexicans as well. Loitering around with his friends and cousins as they were up to no good. Him and his cousins/friends would always go out together on the weekends to have a little fun. Especially in Mexico, where in this carnival you had a little bit more liberty and there was no curfew or a law telling you what to do. Being the teen that my father was he was feeling himself, as he would chill and maybe crack a cold one with his boys no one knew what was bound to come up.

    My father began to dance and started dancing circles around the dudes that came closer to him. My father loved these types of nights, and just going out with his boys and grooving along the beat of the music and all dressed up. He was dress up as kiss, so that meant that he was wearing black leather jeans, with a leather jacket, and with a painted face. Now how intimidating is that? Not really I know right. Well that was just the style and what being cool was like back in the day and when then what had happened is that my father made the other groups angry because they felt some sort of disrespected somehow. They decided to start shoving my dad and then my dad shoved back. So my father's friends and cousin's jumped in and then they began to brawl. Even though none of them decided to hit one another they did shove a lot and they started shouting out a bunch of nonsense. All of a sudden they calmed down and both groups signaled each other as if they were about to have a dance battle and they did. By the way that my father explained it to me, I really wish that I was there to see him, and see how it went down. According to my father he was really hyped and was just feeling himself. He was flipping, sliding, spinning, and doing all sorts of dance moves.

My father said that back in his time he used to be able to breakdance and I believe him. Why would he make a story up like this? My father really said that he felt like a rockstar and he felt as if he was full of joy without wanting to stop dancing. All of a sudden though the other group shot back with dance moves that weren't even solvable. They made no sense, and my dad's group laughed. So he gave them a little piece of his dance moves to show them how it's done and really out do them to get them out of the carnival. Step after step, and spin after spin, my father shut the dance battle down. Especially with his American dance moves that he had told me he had learned from watching videos online. The whole crowd that was on my dad's side was hyped to the music and to the steps that my father was performing, more and more people decided to join in on the action and see what was going on. Everybody around them started yelling and cheering. Obviously now you can tell why my dad felt like a rockstar, because he was a dancing kiss member. How did he do it? I don't know, but I think it's because he is my dad. He tells me every time and is always bragging about how good of a dancer he is. I know he is a good dancer, also he was even bragging about how good of a dancer he was during this interview.

My father sure did miss these times, and just being around his family back in Mexico. He misses everything. He even told me about how he misses his cousins and especially his parents. Wishing that he could've gone back just to prevent himself, or just to not argue and fight with his siblings. He told me how he would have wanted to cherish every single moment that he had with his cousins, brothers, and sisters. He used to fight with them even though now he realizes how much of a bad thing and waste of time that is. My father would have wanted to keep all his memories with them positive. Just because the time went by fast and not everybody in my dad's family is around anymore. Just like his parents they aren't around anymore. I never got a chance to even meet them, and my dad's mom passed away when he was like about twelve years old. He does though remember when him and his family would go out like on some sort of vacation and then they would all enjoy each other and their own hospitality. He told me that he would basically do anything in the world (metaphorically) to just be with his family or relive the past just because of how much he misses it.

Ain't that special? There are so many other things that I found out about my dad during this interview. Although, I don't really think that I have to talk about it or say anything as long as I remember these things and know that I feel closer to him. He told me about all his crazy, goofy, sad, and adventurous stories that I never would have known. My dad did some weird things back in the day, like who dresses like kiss occasionally? Then to find out that he could breakdance! Now that was insane, and I was really surprised at the fact the he used to breakdance. I know my father was and is a good dancer, but breakdancing? Really? Anyways, the interview even got emotional just because he would share his happiest memories and growing up. It was overall a great and successful interview, and my dad is one special dude.

Magic
By Andrea Padilla

What if magic was real for everyone like it is for to me. I've seen magic before. And yes, I am talking about wands and sparkling finger tips. I've seen every kind of magic. I know a magician named Elvis. He wasn't supposed to tell anyone about his magical life. He was short, dark skinned, he had really bushy eyebrows and his nose was a mixture of big and small. I guess you can say he has a medium nose. The type of nose that only looks big from some angles, but is actually a decent size. He had small lips and over that he was growing a mustache. He was also growing a beard from his cleft chin. His ears were pretty big and his hair was long. He had A LOT of facial hair.

  Let me introduce myself. I am Andrea. I am also not so tall. My eyes are a light brown and my eyebrows are thin. I have bags under my eyes because I spend most of my time watching Elvis practice magic rather than sleeping. I also have small lips and a cleft chin. I thought it was cool seeing someone with the same chin as me. I consider cleft chins to be a very unique gene. And I feel that people who inherit it are special, different from others, & one of a kind. I always watched him walk around school alone. I wanted to interact with him. Unfortunately, I was too shy to ever speak.

One day, I was walking home from school, as I listened to Mealting by Cuco in my headphones. It was loud enough to be heard outside of my headphones. As I stopped being less interested in the song, my attention was drawn to a wall. It wasn't just an ordinary wall. I heard activity and movement. But that wasn't the best part. There was sparkles floating in the air through the corner of the wall. I peaked over, and my eyes couldn't believe what I had just seen. "Is that, Elvis?" I asked myself. And I blinked about 20 times just to make sure I wasn't imagining things. I even pinched my arm. He looked so innocent. But as i stood, I saw the same sparkles appear on his fingertips. He stood with one leg forward and one leg back. And he arched his back as he repeated the same spell to a wall. "Wall, turn into a hall!" He repeated that a million times, until the wall turned into an open path. I was confused, shocked, excited. I felt every emotion. I walked closer, and closer. When he saw me, he tried to run. I can tell he was hoping I didn't recognize him. But I did. Of course I did. He tried to run through the path he opened, but his powers were not yet strong enough and the path turned into a wall again and when he tried to run through it, he ran into it. I told him I wouldn't say anything. He couldn't hide or make me unsee what I had already seen.

He told me all about it. As his powers grew, we grew closer. The closer we grew, the more power he gained. Soon enough, he had way too much power in his hands, that he had to pass some on. And so, he passed some down to me. My baggy eyes were no longer there because I enjoyed watching Elvis. Now, they were there because it was me practicing magic all the time. We got so good and what we did, and all our practice payed off. We were now two magicians.

Sew Your Love Into Me
by Marisol Diaz Nunez

Hoseok had always dreamed of what it would be like to meet his soulmate. Will his soulmate like him? Will his soulmate be a nice person? Will his soulmate be a male or female? He doesn't know when it will happen but feels it in his heart, it will happen soon. The stories his mother used to tell him about how she met his dad always gave him hope that he will find his soulmate someday, and fall in love with them. Heavy rain comes down from outside, as the clouds draped over the city, the streets empty with people taking shelter into the warm shops and houses, the soft sounds of the showers are heard from the inside of the warm coffee shop. In the shop, 23 year old, Hoseok rests his head on the counter of the coffee shop, his black hair falls to his eyes as he waits for his time to clock out. As the time reaches out he begins cleaning up when he hears the chiming of the bell from the door, his head reacts to the sound as he looks up he sees a young man, who seems around his age with faded mint hair, walk into the shop completely soaked and cold. "I'm sorry I know you're closed but my house is a bit too far to make it, do you mind if I stay a bit?" The boy looks to be shivering, his lips almost matching his hair. "Of course I don't mind, Let me get you some towels" Hoseok exclaimed feeling worried that his boy may catch a cold. He hurries to the back to get the spare towels, when he feels something tug at his hand. He turns his head eagerly at the boy as he stares at this bright red string before him. A shocked expression also lands on the mint haired boys face, his cheeks grew warm as he look up to meet Hoseok's eyes. "So It's you" he says with smile, "The names Yoongi, Nice to meet you soulmate". Hoseok feels his cheeks grow warm as he tries not to smile so much, to think another male was his soulmate. He feels the string go slightly loose as they seem to have finally connected, the string waits for its time to fade, which should be after a heartfelt connection and acceptance is had. Hoseok sees that Yoongi is still slightly shivering he realized he still need to get the towels. "Oh I'm sorry, let me go get those towel wait here" He exclaimed, Yoongi only slightly laughed while giving him a shy smile, as he sat down on the warm latte brown seats looking at the red knot on his ring finger, that only he and his soulmate will be able to see from now on. The red strings work with only those destined, when a soulmate is found the string shines brightly only fading a few seconds afterwards to the passersby that watched at the right time, but for the ones that are now destined together the string is visible at will. It is a reminder of fate that has lead you your other half. If your soulmate were to pass away before your time of meeting the string breaks forever leaving a broken string at one's finger. Yoongi watched the string grow longer, visibly transparent as Hoseok leaves to get towel. To think would his parents be mind that his soulmate is a man? It not like they are against it but it would be a surprise. He had promised his mother that the moment he finds his soulmate, that he would tell her all about them. His thoughts are broken as he sneezed a storm, he knows for sure he's gonna get sick, at least he has an excuse not to go to work, or school. He just hopes his best friend won't go all mother mode on him again. He starts giggling at the thought of Hoseok meeting his friends, knowing he would fit right in. Most of his friends have soulmates that are also the same gender, which was something they had in common that brought them together as friends. Recently there have been many people finding soulmates of the same gender, so it's no surprise to anyone anymore if your soulmate turn out to be the same gender. He remembered when his childhood friend, Suran, found out her soulmate was the same "cute frozen yogurt girl" she telling him about and how the two are happily living together. He was shocked by the warmth of the baby blue towel that laid on his head "Sorry it took me awhile, I hope you didn't freeze to much" Hoseok smiled as he wrapped another mint green towel on his shoulders wrapping Yoongi in its warmth. "No its fine, Thank you" Yoongi assured him. Hoseok proceed to sit down across from Yoongi looking away with a flushed face. "S-so tell me about yourself?" He asked, Yoongi thought for awhile " I'm 24, I'm from Daegu, I take a music major, and I'm on my last year of college, I like to make music, uh and my favorite color is white." He named off a few main points about himself. He looked up at Hoseok waiting for a response when he noticed the boys sweet smile. He was never really interested in finding his soulmate, in fact at times he would forget that he had a soulmate to find but now that he's right here from of him, he didn't want to let him go, he wanted to know more. This boy had an aura completely opposite of his, but like they say opposites attract. "Well, I'm 23 so that makes you my hyung, I'm from Gwangju, I'm in my second year of college and I take a dance major, I like to dance and my favorite color is green." He beamed his smile almost shaped like a heart, Yoongi could feel the light beaming from Hoseok. Hoseok was relieved that he could become comfortable with his soulmate. They sat there for a while not knowing what else to say, the silence was comfortable, all they wanted to do was enjoy their company. They looked outside as the rain looked to have finally subsided, as the window showed the droplets showered on the streets and building, and the beautiful plants on the outside of the small shop, "Well that was quick, I wonder why it got out of hand earlier?" Yoongi asked looking at his watch checking to see the time only 20 minutes passed by since he got here. "Maybe it was fate" Hoseok chuckles, "Are you always this cheesy?" Yoongi asked as he smiled at the boys word. " I have to go my roommate's probably worried, since I never miss dinner, and his boyfriend is visiting, you busy this week?" Yoongi asked getting out of his seat handing his phone to Hoseok as he entered in his number, "Actually, I'm free right now I just need to close the shop, I mean if you want to go on a date another time it's fine" Hoseok explained. "No actually if you're free right now, mind joining me as my date to dinner, I don't wanna third wheel anymore, besides I'm sure my friends would like to meet you, only if you want of course?" Yoongi offered. " I would love to join you, soulmate!" Hoseok cheered as he grabbed his belongings in his bag, grabbing his keys while following Yoongi to the door locking it. He turns to Yoongi as he noticed him holding his hand out, the one with the red string. "Wanna hold hands, I won't take no for an answer" Yoongi demanded. Hoseok laughed at Yoongi's boldness, walking next to him intertwining their hands together, while the string lit brightly.

Through The Eyes Of A Mother
By Marisol Diaz Nunez

My mother is an interesting women. At first glance with her green beautiful eyes filled with joy, underneath it all is more to life than meets the eyes. To me she is the best mother in the world, of course we have ups and down but a mother is an irreplaceable thing. I liked to think I knew everything about my mother, but one fateful night I knew everything and held the secrets she once held before.

Let's start at the beginning before I was even born, her childhood I was never told much about it, only small stories of how she lived and how you lived freely outside in the world unlike today she reminds me. Like when her mother used to make her and her sister little tea pots out of clay, and beautiful dolls that they held so dear. Let's start off with something important my mom grew up with 7 other siblings she has 8 in total but one came way later in their life. She would tell me stories of her home place, she would talk about the how the stars glowed at night, and how the neighborhood kids would play all day and all night till their moms called out to them to come home to eat, cause as my mom likes to remind me there weren't any phones back then.

Let me tell you more about her teenage years, years I relate the most to her, she tells me about how back then she used to be a rebel, savage, wouldn't take anything from anyone who messed with her, she was well known in her town for beating up people that would mess with her family. The family name Nunez was a big, known, name its prime beign when my great great grandfather was well known for killing men who would abuse their wives he was a respected man killed by betrayal, due to wanting to mess with purely our family name. This name was very famous in the pueblo, I don't to say it was feared but it was pretty well known.

Today my mother is loud and aggressive but she is the sweetest most funnest person to talk to, she doesn't hold back on her opinion, maybe that's why she was so popular. There were many problems between her family, at least between her parents, mainly her dad they had many arguments, and incidents that I won't share, but soon after she decided to marry someone, who is now my father whom she loves so much, though they were married by contract, they knew each other as acquaintances, but wanted to help each other out. Throughout the years though they slowly fell in love and changed for each other.

Soon after my brother was born, but my father wasn't always the best, I personally don't want to get into details but from what my mother has told me that before they would fight a lot, and that things were bad to the point she was close to leaving. Then everything changed when I was born. That is what I was told, I don't know why, but I am glad I was able to change a life.

I'm Not Sorry
By Abraham Esqueda

You gotta let me know if If I can be your whole sin
Only tell you real shit, that's the tea no sip

Don't trip, Don't trip, that money tricky, no whip
We ain't spending on shit, we just sippin' on this

Just forget the whole mess, pretend like it was nothin
I impregnate your mind, lets have a baby without fuckin,
and

You tried to play nice, everybody just took advantage
You left your fridge open,
somebody just took a sandwich, and

Why you take it as a game, you just gon lose yo energy
Congrats you played yourself and just became the enemy

You see all of a sudden you stopped fuckin with me
But baby what if you never lost your faith in me

I can't get no rest I, I lie around with my tech
Waiting for a response, I feel like a fucking test

So is it just me, or is it life and it's savagery
If it ain't me release my mind and set it free

You out here treating me, as if the blames on me
And you take shots at me,
and got me feeling like Kennedy

I don't know but hanging out with you is a no go
Changed the feeling and made the mood a no more

Yo lifes so lovely, you say you see me and I say barely
I make you feel shitty with your worries,
it's funny but I'm not sorry

My Mom's Perfume
By Kylie Cazares

I remember a lot of things from when I was young.
I remember going to the park in the late afternoons
to play with my friends
while my dad would play football with his.
I remember spending the night at people's houses
When there were huge and loud parties.
I remember always brushing
my tia's soft and blonde hair.
I remember the times I've spent with my mom.

When I was just a small child,
I would watch my mom get ready for work.
Seeing her put a black outfit on showing some skin.
I would ask,
Are you going to work mommy?
She would look at me through the mirror and nod.
I see her curling her hair carefully with the curling iron.
I'd ask,
Do you have to look pretty mommy?
She would reply with a soft tone
and a comforting smile saying yes.
I'd see her put perfume on.
I asked,
Can you spray me mommy?

She turned to me with her rose colored spray

with glitter mixed with it.
She told me to raise my arms up.
I formed my arms into a T form.
She told me to close my eyes tight.
I squinched my whole face and held my breath.

She sprayed me four times.
Once on top.
Once on both sides of my body.
And once on my lower half.
I smelled sweetness.
Specifically a light scent of peach,
Mixed with a hint of huckleberry
And a scent of roses.

But sadly I forgot to close my mouth.
The taste wasn't as good as the scent.
It was almost like the taste of soap.
Or like the taste of orange juice after you've brushed your teeth.
My reaction made my mother laugh,
She would sound almost like a donkey and a monkey.

I smiled then ran off to play with my brother.
I remember a lot from my childhood.
It's mostly the happy moments.
The fun moments.
I even remember the smell of my mom's perfume.

Part Three
ANCHORS

This I Believe About the Afterlife
By Bryan Herrera

I believe that all of us will die one day all of us will dug underneath the ground. I believe that there is an after life when we die. There will be gateway to heaven and we will all live a happy and wondrous life as someone new. When we die there will be no more racism no more discrimination. So why is that now we argue with one another want to fight one another and racist towards each other, if one day we will just die. I believe that our men and women who fight for our country just die to to see us behave they fight for our country so that we can be safe from people who don't lie us. I believe that we need to stand up together and stand up for one another because we will all die one day and when we reach the heavens doors we shall all live to one another no matter what race we are. I believe that one day God will come down and save everyone who knows how to love one another and will rise people up from the dead because they are good people who sinned but learned from their mistakes and fix them quick

    I believe that all this inequality shit needs to stop this isn't how we should be living. We should be happy that we live on this earth and we should be thankful that when we die there will be an afterlife where there will be no problems in that afterlife that we live good and we will see everything good. I believe that the people we kill and the people who we miss treat will have a better life then the person who killed them those people will not be able to see the afterlife in heaven they will be somewhere else down in a volcano where is deep and very dark and scarey where at the end of the volcano you see two red beady eyes. I believe that everyone who is racist and someone who thinks they are the most powerful and are very special because they have a lot of money, well they aren't special because none of that money will go with them anywhere it will be left behind for his kids.Once you lose all your money ur useless and you won't even have a voice any more.

I believe that once we all see that we are all the same we all hurt the same we all have the same feelings we will see that money will not make us any more different we can all have nice things if people wouldn't be hateful towards each other and racist. We as a society should be helping one another get to the top and not be greedy we shall believe that once we all die we will see God with his arms wide open hugging us all for everything we have done to help one another get to the to.

The Truth
By Carlos Lainez

I believe with the last one and the reason for that is because I need proof that there there is a god because my parent are the one that encourages me to believe in god. Recently I went on my own and stopped listening to them about god and tried to ignore every topic they've bring up that involves god because every time I say something about that they keep adding why god is good and why he's "real" which when I was little I was going through rough times and they've told me to pray for things to get better. I was stupid enough to listen to that and every time I did I expected something to change something to happen but nothing happened and so I stopped listening to them because I thought it was a lie and it actually turned out to be a lie because they say to pray for things to become better. That was a lie because they told me things will turn out better but they didn't it was just a big lie and that parents make you follow because I feel like everyone that believe in a religion they were encouraged by their parent or someone close to them or unless you are like someone that like is really interested into god but myself I believe that there is no god.

The reason I say that because a long time ago I struggled a lot with things I prayed and I prayed and nothing happened that's when I started to believe that he wasn't real. The thing is that it's weird that my family that

I don't believe in god because like my uncles and parent are like religious and like in family gathering like dinners etc.. They would say grace and like I was the only one that wasn't in it and that felt weird because like everyone kept their eyes closed and held each other's hands. Then when I tried to eat when I was hungry they didn't let me because it was disrespectful to whoever is saying grace so they wouldn't let me eat because of that I found that dumb because they didn't let me eat and I was hungry so like every time I touched my food they didn't let me eat but recently when every time they did that I started eating and like they haven't told me anything and so it was whatever to them about it.

It's funny how Parents encourage things that aren't real but aye it isn't the first time they lied about things being real for example SANTA, TOOTH FAIRY. Finally all besides that I believe that there is no god. I also believe that I shouldn't be judged on that topic because I know that there are some people that judge you for not believe but I myself have respect for the people who believe in god I never say nothing to them because they have the rights to their own beliefs and I have mine so I respect them.

The Wandering Girl
By Marisol Diaz Nunez

I'm tired things aren't the same. I'm tired of it, why can't things be the same like they were before. Was it because of me? It's almost as if I'm not here, but they still look my way. I wonder why did things change, I don't get it, but I'll keep trying to make things go back to how they were, to when we were a happy family. I see the dining table chair pulled out from the table. The table still has an untouched plate, with my favorite food, I go to sit on it as a way to not make too much noise. I watch my Mom watching T.V. though she looks the same, her eyes share a different feeling, as if she's been hurt. As if she lost something important. I wonder what it is, hopefully I can find it.

    I get up from where I'm sitting I watch my Dad pass by my Mom to head outside in the backyard, away from the gloomy atmosphere. He's probably gonna feed the dogs.I watch him open the glass door, leaving it open. I walk out with him "Juan cierra la puerta, hace frio"(-Juan close the door, it's cold) I hear my Mom exclaim. I follow him to where the two Golden Retrievers were, I watch as he fills their bowls with food. I get close enough to the fence when I hear the dog bark at me. Startled, I jump away with a yelp, "Guerro no es nada, no me asustes"(Guerro it's nothing, don't scare me like that) my Dad scolds the dog, I giggle slightly. I wanted to move closer again when I see my brother, Dorian, walk out of the garage, which is his small room, right behind him along with our two small yorkie dogs.

My Dad also noticed him "Como estas, quieres comer, tenemos pozole"(How've you been, you hungry we have pozole?) He asked, Dorian only looked down with a made up smile "No, no tengo hambre,"(No I'm not hungry) he says my dad doesn't seem to believe him but he doesn't say more "Okay, pero por favor no se te olvide comer,"(Okay but please don't forget to eat) my dad tells him as he nodded. 'Could it be the bills that are stressing them out, maybe I should get a part time job to help'. He excused himself as he walked back into the room, I follow along with Tweety and Kookie, who finished playing outside. I sit down on the small couch, his room walls filled with posters of the shows we used to watch, and the video games he plays, and the drawing I drew him of a cool spider chick. I smile as I always feel proud of that drawing seeing it on his wall. 'I'm glad he likes it'. I turn to look at him, but he ignores me, almost as if he's mad. 'I wonder why he's mad, maybe that's the reason why he doesn't want to hang out with me anymore'.

I hear the door open, it's my Mom who probably came by to ask him to eat leaving the door wide open. I decide to walk out as I noticed I was ignored by her. 'Doesn't she care that I'm hungry too'. I see the glass door open too, so I walk in as tears threatened to fill my eyes, the weather lady was wrong again it seems. I'm still wearing my favorite "Stray Kids" sweater and black leggings too, I've been wearing the same thing for a few days now. I use the sleeves of my sweater to wipe my eyes as I walk to my room I see the door is closed and It almost looks as if it hasn't been opened for weeks. I turn the knob of the door, it's slightly jammed like always, I felt like I almost passed through it.

My room looks untouched, the bed still as messy as ever. I go up to pick up my favorite stuffed animal, which is a cute seal pillow pet, the one my Mom gave me as a gift years ago. I place it down on the bed again, I looked up at my drawing on the walls, mainly BTS and Kpop drawings, with other realistic work. I smile at my work and the progress that can be seen in each one. I walk out, I see my mom looking at the photos from my elementary school days, and the photos from my volleyball team. I smile remembering my Mom's cheers at the games she attended and how she would give me advice on how to be better next time, but she doesn't smile instead an ocean of tears start to fill her eyes. My smile fades, I want to hug her, but I fear she will only reject me, I watch my Dad wrap his arms around her along with almost invisible tears, his tears are silent. What did I do? Did I disappoint them?

They move to the living room, as my Mom wiped her tears, the news turned on to the follow up of the recent story. I hear the news anchor begin to speak "A young girl, has unfortunately passed away a few days ago, after being shot on her way home from school, witnesses say the girl was caught in the gunfire with younger students who were also caught in the gunshots, fortunately the small group of kids were unharmed, but the victim that was killed has been identified as Marisol Diaz a young sophomore, attending the nearby school, our hearts go out to this young girl and her family as well".

'I guess it was my fault'

This One's For You
By Emely Alarcon

Ericka Alarcon: 5'0, fair skin, colored eyes mostly green with little bits of brown in them, black straight hair, dark eyebrows. This is my mom. Born in Guatemala on January 16, 1984, she was raised by her mother, father, 5 other siblings. An average morning for her was to wake up early make the tortillas serve her father and her brothers food before they went off to work, clean the house, and gather up all the dirty laundry from the house and go wash clothes at the pound that was like 4 blocks away, and wash clothes. She would have to do all this before going to school, but she still managed to be positive about her life. Growing up she said she felt, "Happy, I loved mom a lot I always helped her." She was very content with her life she didn't complain a lot even though she grew up barely having anything.

    The best time of the year for her was her birthday and independence day. Her birthday because that's when she was able to show off her new clothes that she got, which was a pair of new shoes and 2 new dresses. She would get these on her birthday which was why she liked her birthday so much. On independence day there would be a party at school " At the parties we would dance, do little comedy skits, they would have topical food that was from Guatemala, this was the only party I could go to because my parents wouldn't let me go out." her father was very strict and didnt let her do much so when she would go out it was a big deal for her.

She grew up having 4 best friends that she considered her sisters she would go to school with them, and spend any free time she had with them. Until one of her closest friend passed away. She was diagnosed with leukemia and passed away in 2004, she was 23 when she passed away. "I never got the chance to say goodbye to her because I was here in the US and by the time I went back she had already passed away, I still see her in my dreams and I sometimes feel like i'm actually talking to her."

Her father was a farmer and her mother would to a lot of things to get money she would make clothes and sell them, she would sell her animal like pigs and chickens, she would also make lunches and would sell them to the men that were working. She would do anything to make money and sometimes they didn't have much because there was a bad harvest or they didnt sell a lot. But she didn't really care about money all she cared about was that she was happy and that she only need her necessities. She was very content with life she didn't let the things she didn't have affect her. She didn't live in a big house, the house she lived in was only two bedroom and she had to share it with her siblings. They didn't have a bathroom either but so did most people that lived there. But one day her mom saved up and made a big kitchen for her because that's where she would spend all her time at. "She cared a lot about the kitchen the kitchen was like her bedroom she would spend all day in the kitchen the only reason she left was to go to sleep otherwise she would have slept in the kitchen." But she always made sure that her kids have everything they needed. They never starved or never looked dirty they always looked clean because her mother was a little of a clean freak and need everything to be spotless still to this day.

When she was six years old when she first went to the capital, "The city was full of lights i've never seen so many lights all in one place like that in my life." Because where she lived it was just a little town nothing compared to the capital. Her older sister took her to the zoo where they had," the most amazing hot dog." They spent almost the whole day there she was having so much fun she never wanted to leave. She went to where her sister lived and it way more different from where she came from there were alot of cars, and were she was from people who had cars were really rich most people got around by horse and they still kinda do to this day. There was no dirt roads, there was big buildings, everything was just way more different. She loved it and when she was older she wanted to live in the capital and have a creer and support her family. Her sister offered her to pay for her school and move with her but her father didn't let her. She was too little and need to be with her family. She only got up to a 6th grade education and she had to drop out because they couldn't afford to pay for more school. But that didn't end up stopping her she came to the US with her husband with not really anything at all, there was a time were they were poor and didn't have much, but they still managed to get out of it. She had her three kids and managed to own multiple properties, nice car, and a house.

Explaining My Happiest to My Mom
By Elvis Arias

Mom, my happiest is you,
Thanks for being a great friend of mind,
I adore you, I care about you I hope I am the best
Son you ever wanted. I am always happy when I get
To see you everyday mom, I am glad I get to call
You my mom. I wish you had the energy you used
To have when you were chasing me,
And playing with me,
When I was little. Miss those times mom.

Leonardo Da Vinci
By Angel Ferracin

Jesus and others sitting in a table having a meal,
everyone looking at Jesus in shock.
Reason everyone is looking at Jesus in a shocked way is
because he told them, "This is my last meal."
Everyone was wondering what he meant by that.
Some told each other, "What does he mean?",
"He's crazy!", "Whatttt?"
After the picture was taken everyone got up and left,
while Jesus stayed there alone and ate his last meal…

Change My Mind
By Marizela Montalvo

I don't even know how to explain the way I feel. Maybe he isn't even real. I feel like if I say something wrong I might get punished but at the same time I don't know if he can even hear. I want to say I do believe in him but there's a little voice in my head that tells me otherwise. Yeah, I pray almost every night, sometimes I forget and when I wake up I beat myself up about it. It makes me feel like i'm ungrateful because I didn't give thanks to him. I sit up on the corner of my bed and just think and think and think. How come atheist don't get punished, a few of my friends are atheist and they seem to be living a normal life like mine. Then I can just already imagine my grandma getting mad at me for even thinking that way. My grandma always comes to mind when this topic comes up. If she were to ever read this, she'd be extremely heartbroken.

    Sometimes when she forces me to go to church with her, I just sit on those hard wooden benches and try to process everything and comprehend what the priest is saying. Its rare when I do understand just some parts of what they're saying and reading. I haven't gone to church since early August when I was in Mexico and I'll be honest the only reason why I went was because I know my grandma would be happy and she would let me go out afterwards. I've listened to so many of her stories and how God does wonders and all this and I can't help but to ask her millions of questions.

There are so many different stories, which one is true? Which one do I believe? I've heard so many outcomes, some don't even make any type of sense. Most of me says to believe it so for now, I'm just going to go with it. Plus, I don't want to disappoint my grandma and make her feel like she taught me nothing because in reality she taught me a lot about the Catholic religion. I've gone to many different churches around the world and they're really beautiful and interesting. I still haven't seen any evidence but I'm just going to go with what my grandma says and pretend like I actually know what is going on.

Guadalupe
By Jaquelyn Martinez

Guadalupe is a 66 year old man who has worked construction for a majority of his life. He had come to the United States to find a better paying job so he could bring out his family and support them. He had one child and his wife. He traveled all around the U.S. until he found a stable job in Florida.

Guadalupe moved to Florida and started working right away. After a few months of earning money he went back to Chihuahua to get his wife and child and take them to their new home. After having lived there a few years he and his wife, Lidu, had three more children. After that everyday was the same routine. Wake up, go to work, come home, eat and sleep, but one day his routine got switched up.

Lidu one day had let the neighbor come over while her husband was at work, little did she know this would be a big mistake. The neighbor was very friendly and "curious" in what they had in their house. The neighbor grabbed some scissors Lidu had in her closet for sewing. Seeing these scissors the neighbor called the cops and told them that LiduVina had an armed weapon in the house. By the time Guadalupe got home the cops were there waiting for him. They were tough on Guadalupe, they grabbed him and forcefully took him out of the house in front of his kid, and didn't even get to say goodbye or anything. They just deported him right then and there.

A few days went by until Guadalupe was back in the states. But by the time he was back he had lost his job, and was on the verge of losing his home. So Guadalupe went out to Las Vegas where he knew the construction was good. He took his wife and four kids.

This time when he came out, not only did he get more money and get a nice house. He also got his papers and got his wife papers so they could no longer be deported. Things were going great, he was working, his wife was working, and he was doing better than ever. His children started growing up and asking him "what kept you trying to come back" and Guadalupe always said " the money and ability to support my family out here".

To this day he and his family are living in Las Vegas. His children have a great education and a good life, thanks to their father risking everything for his children. They have nice houses, good paying jobs and more. Guadalupe is now retired and living life without a worry, and his wife is still working and living happily with her husband. Now he tells his grandchildren his stories of his many "adventures" as a young man traveling the United States looking for his future.

El Moises Barragan: A Tribute
By Manuel M.

Born September 28, 2001, his grandpa never thought
That would be his only son
Having 4 daughters and 1 angel
He lived his life drinking the pain away
Working with cement
and blocks he didn't just have mental pain but also
Physical pain
The drinking and heavy work made him go through a
path that he never thought he'd go through
One day he fell hard to the ground his eyes closed,
He woke up in a room with very bright lights,
and a woman calling him
"Moises are you okay?"
He responded with a yes
He would have never imagined he would be
In and out the hospital for the next 3 years
Being diagnosed with kidney failure and heart failure
Doctors made him into an animal
An animal that they would be experimenting on
for the rest of
His Life.

He Can't Say Goodbye
By Angel Ferracin

He's living and he always will. Never will he die. Years past, people are dying, others are being born and he's still there. New family all the time, his siblings' kids are his nephews and nieces, then their kids are too, then their kids, and it goes on forever. He's never alone. 30 year old man who can never die, ten years pass and he's still 30. Another ten years pass and he's still 30. His kids now 20, not knowing there father is still 30, thinking he's fifty, he never tells them or anyone. He's living forever, but only he knows. 65 years later, his kids are dying and he's still thirty. Watching his kids all wrinkly and old, shatters his heart. Watching the death of his kids is killing him and he wants to die. He tries committing suicide multiple times but he just won't die. He hates it and wishes nothing but to die.

Part Four
DEEP DARK WATER

Dream of the Forest
By Kevin Hernandez

Some time ago, there was an enormous woodland with numerous types of trees. In that backwoods carries on a mother goat and her little sheep. They were cheerfully living in the backwoods. The naughty sheep. The mother goat thought that it was hard to take care of her kids, The Naughty Lamb.

The shadiness of the sheep found no limits. This was the issue of the mother goat. The mother goat felt stressed. Their house was close to the edge of the backwoods. In that area, there were numerous hunters.
One day, The Naughty Lamb wandered into the woods. He enjoyed taking a swivel at the tall trees and stunning blooms all of a sudden he realized that he lost his direction. "Oh my Goodness I have come far from home. Mother will be furious with me" he thought

Out of little sheep's sight, there was a wolf who was viewing from behind a tree. "Yummy! That sheep is precisely what I need for my lunch today," he started, licking his lips in a ferocious way.

The wolf sprint towards the sheep accepting his sharp teeth stated, "A little alike like try not to get into this mysterious woods. I am here going to have you for my lunch today."
The little delicate sheep was in panicked. He

stopped for a minute, without recognizing where he was or what to do. At that point, he picked up his fearlessness ass, returned and kept running as quick as possible. The wolf took after nearly grasping him. The little sheep kept running at her most extreme speed, for quite a while. The wolf took after.

In the interim, the mother goat not discovering her tyke the little sheep at home was stressed. "I trust he has not gone into the woodland. I should go and search for him," she thought.

So additionally as she would get into the thick woodland, she saw the little sheep leaving the perilous backcountry. He was gasping and there was a wolf looking for after behind the little sheep. The mother goat utilizing her long horns looked for after the cunning wolf away into the forested zones.

The mother goat kept running behind the wolf for some separation into the woods and ended up guaranteed that the wolf would not come back again into the adjacent territories of their home. After the mother goat returned to their home, it saw that the little sheep was shuddering in fear. Mother goat took him inside their home and when he quieted the little one, stated, "Now, I trust you have learnt a lesson that the woods isn't the place for goats like us." The little sheep just gestured. The little goat never went to the timberland. After this occurrence, both the mother and her kid goat lived cheerfully for quite a while.

Lovesick
By Marizela Montalvo

I'm missing you so much
More than ever before.
It sucks that you're not around anymore.
My love for you was galore
Apparently you didn't want it anymore.
The thought of you being with someone else makes my stomach turn.
Not only am i lovesick
But homesick as well
Being in your arms was home to me
And now i'm wishing that i was home right now.
I got use to your own, unique scent.
whenever you came around
it felt as if i lit a candle into flame.
The comfort of your arms around me
Felt like a blanket wrapped around me.
I can't help but to be lonely without you.
I have your name spinning in my mind
Up until i cry
And then i don't know what to do.
I can't even think straight
Without you constantly on my mind.
I'm not going to lie
You really impacted my life.

This One's For You
By Emely Alarcon

Ericka Alarcon: 5'0, fair skin, colored eyes mostly green with little bits of brown in them, black straight hair, dark eyebrows. This is my mom. Born in Guatemala on January 16, 1984, she was raised by her mother, father, 5 other siblings. An average morning for her was to wake up early make the tortillas serve her father and her brothers food before they went off to work, clean the house, and gather up all the dirty laundry from the house and go wash clothes at the pound that was like 4 blocks away, and wash clothes. She would have to do all this before going to school, but she still managed to be positive about her life. Growing up she said she felt, "Happy, I loved mom a lot I always helped her." She was very content with her life she didn't complain a lot even though she grew up barely having anything.

      The best time of the year for her was her birthday and independence day. Her birthday because that's when she was able to show off her new clothes that she got, which was a pair of new shoes and 2 new dresses. She would get these on her birthday which was why she liked her birthday so much. On independence day there would be a party at school " At the parties we would dance, do little comedy skits, they would have topical food that was from Guatemala, this was the only party I could go to because my parents wouldn't let me go out." her father was very strict and didnt let her do much so when she would go out it was a big deal for her.

She grew up having 4 best friends that she considered her sisters she would go to school with them, and spend any free time she had with them. Until one of her closest friend passed away. She was diagnosed with leukemia and passed away in 2004, she was 23 when she passed away. "I never got the chance to say goodbye to her because I was here in the US and by the time I went back she had already passed away, I still see her in my dreams and I sometimes feel like i'm actually talking to her."

Her father was a farmer and her mother would to a lot of things to get money she would make clothes and sell them, she would sell her animal like pigs and chickens, she would also make lunches and would sell them to the men that were working. She would do anything to make money and sometimes they didn't have much because there was a bad harvest or they didnt sell a lot. But she didn't really care about money all she cared about was that she was happy and that she only need her necessities. She was very content with life she didn't let the things she didn't have affect her. She didn't live in a big house, the house she lived in was only two bedroom and she had to share it with her siblings. They didn't have a bathroom either but so did most people that lived there. But one day her mom saved up and made a big kitchen for her because that's where she would spend all her time at. "She cared a lot about the kitchen the kitchen was like her bedroom she would spend all day in the kitchen the only reason she left was to go to sleep otherwise she would have slept in the kitchen." But she always made sure that her kids have everything they needed. They never starved or never looked dirty they always looked clean because her mother was a little of a clean freak and need everything to be spotless still to this day.

When she was six years old when she first went to the capital, "The city was full of lights i've never seen so many lights all in one place like that in my life." Because where she lived it was just a little town nothing compared to the capital. Her older sister took her to the zoo where they had," the most amazing hot dog." They spent almost the whole day there she was having so much fun she never wanted to leave. She went to where her sister lived and it way more different from where she came from there were alot of cars, and were she was from people who had cars were really rich most people got around by horse and they still kinda do to this day. There was no dirt roads, there was big buildings, everything was just way more different. She loved it and when she was older she wanted to live in the capital and have a creer and support her family. Her sister offered her to pay for her school and move with her but her father didn't let her. She was too little and need to be with her family. She only got up to a 6th grade education and she had to drop out because they couldn't afford to pay for more school. But that didn't end up stopping her she came to the US with her husband with not really anything at all, there was a time were they were poor and didn't have much, but they still managed to get out of it. She had her three kids and managed to own multiple properties, nice car, and a house.

Hellevator
By Esmeralda Arroyo

As I roam the streets of the city, I listen to my favorite music with my earbuds on. While the music revolves in my mind, I've figured out that my surroundings have gone silent. I continue to walk slowly, but suddenly come to a stop and everything in front of me stays in their place. The people around me stopped in their tracks, birds still in the air with their wings open and cars waiting for the green light to go on. I observe each person which I imagine as trees, making me want to touch their rough exterior, break a piece of bark and reveal their untold stories.

     I grab ahold of my earbud and pull it out of my ear. I stay there for a second, with the earbud still in hand, and everything starts to move into motion. People start to stroll down the sidewalks, birds glide in the air, and cars beep at each other. I frown and look at the earbud held tightly in my hands. I figured out that you can't get rid of reality with just a simple earbud. I thought I could live without choosing a path. Instead of choosing a path, I chose a twist of a never ending maze.

     At the end of this maze was an elevator, a hellevator. It's too late to run away, I'm on the hellevator and I can't do anything, but stand inside. I grab ahold of the earbud, put it back into my ear, press the button that says HELL, and close my eyes, waiting to arrive to a dark tunnel of nothingness.

Lemonade
By Noah Baldridge

Yesterday life gave me lemons
Vile, rotted, lemons
And we all know what to do when life gives you lemons,
You make lemonade,
Lemonade is cliche,
Instead,
Today,
I say no thank you,
Not today

Emotionally jumped,
Stomp out on the cold concrete
Shards of lie and deceit jab into me
it was my fault though,
Butting my head into something i shouldn't even know,
me being me,
couldn't take my head out of my ass,
didn't read the instructions
Added too much sugar
Made their relationship sour
All i said is that i'm here and i care,
that's it,
I don't care
last time i did you deprived me of air,
Choking, clinging to life
wanted you as a wife

choking, clinging to you
When i'm with you i forget what to do
You were my everything
Well,
You still are
Something to quench my thirst in these hellish days
Yet
When trying to reach out to you
You just give me a disapproving stare while i grasp at the air

The one who promised you to me vandalised his promise
Instead,
He used me to get closer to you
I don't blame him though
Your sugar sweet taste could get anyone hooked
Ive known you since 4th grade man
Yet time is meaningless
So how could i expect you to care

Now i see her daily
Heartbreak clotting in my veins
It's like a bitter sweet aftertaste
Unique only to you
Sweet lemonade

Utah
By Noah Baldridge

Met a girl first months of my life,
Thought we'd be together forever,
Perfect wife.
Mormon girl,
Goody two shoes,
I was young,
Always hurt, but she was there to kiss my boo boos.

I loved her from the very start,
She was so cold though,
She left me with a frostbitten heart,

Like permafrost,
She's never left my head,
I've always loved her, but at what cost?

I'm with a new girl now,
She treats me right,
Even though we sometimes fight,
She's all sunshine and rainbows.

But ya know,
I've always prefered the snow.

Nyx
By Esmeralda Arroyo

In the witching hour, the clouds covered the glowing lantern that lit up the sky. The visible cloud water droplets covered all of the king's domain.

Bladed weapons were pointed towards the prince. Nyx held her sword towards the traitors, protecting the prince. She didn't know whether to take the traitors or the princes side since she was both. Her mind was thinking about her father's words,"You're not the princes friend. You're nothing but a sidekick to him".

Slowly, her sword turned towards the prince, right next to his neck. The prince was shocked towards her actions and turned to face her. Her sturdy hands grabbed firm of the sword, waiting for what was going to happen next.

"I'm sorry Your Highness, but…" Nyx said, slowly bowing towards the prince. "BUT WHAT!", the prince had a cold stern look on his face, clenching his teeth together. He was raging with anger, but was weeping on the inside.

"I don't know if I should be called your friend or should I just remain as your sidekick", Nyx said with her head held low.

The prince was surprised by her choice of words and understood what she meant to say.

"I'm sorry I never noticed this, but you will always be someone I care about. If I had to trust someone, in this whole entire world, it will be you. You're the one I can count on. Even if you betray me, I will trust in what you say to me. You have your reasons as well, it's not always going to be about me". The princes words made Nyx look up at him with a thankful smile which also made the prince grin.

His grin slowly turned into a frown as Nyx tried to put her sword down. "Dont! You'll get shot if you put it down. Just leave it how it is", the prince said with his hand pulling the sword next to his neck. Nyx just grabbed the princes hand and pulled it off the sword. She had put the sword down.

CLANK!

All arrows point towards her and is shot in less than a second. She slowly falls to the ground on her knees, arrows still flying towards her. The wine-colored blood appears on her abdomen and shoulder. Her body laid flat on the dusty floor.

"STOP!"

The prince yells, drops down to his knees and pulls her close to him. "NO! Nyx wake up!",eyes filled with sadness and tears dropping out of his eyes. Nyx's eyes began to flutter open, "I will always consider you as my friend".

I'm Straight
By Jacob Sellers

I realized my sexuality younger than most people do, I was in the first grade of elementary school when this girl asked me to be her friend and I said sure her name was Alexis she was pale girl with light brown hair and a set of sky blue eyes. I later on started seeing her as cute and I liked her but I was too small to know much about how dating and all this boyfriend/girlfriend stuff worked so I just treated her nicely and shared everything with her. I thought she was pretty and had a great personality I liked how she would always share her cryans with me and sat next to me when it was drawing time. I told my mom about how I liked this girl at school and she asked me about her and I described her, my mom was proud of me and that made me proud for myself. This encounter changed my perspective on life and opened my eyes to the world of women.

After this it wasn't hard at all to realize my attraction to girls, ever since i've always had a crush on some girl even if it was small crush. I always liked women and always will too, I guess it just sparked in me to realize that there is a whole new lifestyle in front of me. This started my journey as a real boy but things become a little different as I grew up and matured. You start finding other things in girls that you never noticed about them, as you grow up and they do to it just gets better and better. In elementary I only saw beauty and personality in girls, I wanted the girls that were nice to me and that their looks fit to my personal appeal which also has changed over time. As I matured and became a teen things change a little in what I looked for a girl, I started noticing things in girls that I never payed attention to when I was younger if you know what I mean. I began to notice these things around middle school and above, as the girls start becoming teens, things change like my view on women are a bit different. I started looking for ass and other body parts more than personality, my priorities change a little and what I wanted in a women went from 1. looks 2.personality to 1. body and looks then 2. personality. Its sad but it's true i'm just being honest here I began looking for lust over love, but that doesn't mean i'm not loyal I just like what girls have and I think that is a huge plus of being straight. What i'm trying to say is that even though I think body is a major part in a women it doesn't mean that I am some kind of fuckboy I still look for a good personality. Also I have noticed that my personal preference has changed on women by race, I used to be into white girls more than any others now my preference in latinas. I feel that race is a big part of a women because of their culture likings are similar to mine, for example I like Mexican music and so do other latina girls so that effects the how I feel about those girls.   I have always had a strong opinion on my sexualality I know that i'm straight and i'm proud of it, I never tried anything else and (no hard feelings to anyone) I never will. That's just how I feel, I know that other people feel different about that especially nowadays that there are a lot of gay right movements and gay marriage is legal now.

Baba Yaga
By Kylie Cazares

There is a tale of a witch that lived deep in the forest. They say that she was able to take form of an ugly, elderly woman; or that she would show an appearance of a young and beautiful lady. There were times when she would either help guide the people she'd come across on their journeys, if she was to get something out of it, or make their lives more miserable.

She was also able to tell folks that passed by about their future, like how they would die. She was known to eat children for breakfast as a nutritional diet. Baba Yaga didn't hate everyone she met though, there were certain types of people that she liked. People who were vulnerable yet intelligent. And those who were asked where they learned how to use magic, they would reply saying Baba Yaga taught them.

It was a dim, the trunks of the trees were dark as if they were burnt. The leafs on the branches were dry and dead. It was quiet, there was a soft breeze that made a whistle, it was almost soundless. Elora's footsteps was the only sound you could hear from a distance. The cracks she made with every step on the leaves that laid dead on the cold floor. Each step that she took, a teardrop would fall.

It felt like she was walking for hours, her feet were sore, her legs were weak, she felt that at any moment her legs would give up and collapse. But somehow, they still managed to take that extra step. Elora doesn't remember how she ended up here, the only remembers going to sleep in her bed and waking up in the middle of this shady forest.

"Hush, little one, sleep." Elora begins to sing a song that her mother use to sing to her as a child. "Don't lie close to the bed edge." She takes another step. "Hush, little one, sleep." Another teardrop. "Wolves howl at the moon." Step. "Hurry to fall asleep." Step. "Hush, little one, bye-bye. Fall asleep soon." She finally falls to her knees. Her legs have given up on her, she laid on the ground motionless. Elora languorously moves her hand against the wet leaves on the floor. "So cold." She said in a soft tone.

"Hush, little one, sleep." Elora hears an old woman's voice in the distance. "Wolves howl at the moon." Elora starts to wonder who was singing the same song.

"Help." Elora says. But her voice was still weak and quiet.

"Don't lie close to the bed edge!" The woman sang, making her voice be heard clearly from miles away. Elora tries to get up and search for the woman, but her legs weren't strong enough to stand on their own.

"Help." Elora tries to scream again, but it was no use. She dragged herself to the nearest tree. She could still hear the old woman's voice in the distance singing that familiar song.

"Hush, little one, sleep! Don't lie to close to the bed!" The woman yelled in the distance.

"Hush, little one, sleep."

"Hush, little one, sleep."

Elora began to sing along with the lady. Tired, but unable to sleep.

"The wolves howl at the moon."

"The wolves howl at the moon."

Suddenly, the woman's singing stops. Elora looks around, "Help," she says in a weak tone, "Come back." She plays the song over and over again in her head, for years she's known that song. And never once did she wonder what it meant. She felt her eyes getting heavy, she started to drift off to sleep peacefully. She plays the song again in her head once more. "Hush, little one, sleep." A soft voice begins to sing.

New Cat in the Hood
By Steve Arroyo

Walking straight down the neighborhood, I came across a new kid in the block. Creased jeans, freshly ironed shirt, and pearl white shoes... I knew I had to get his name because it was always like that with new cats here.

"Yo, you new G?" I asked, even though I already knew.

"Yeah homeboy, just moved in this hood this morning, what's good?" said the new cat.

"Nun, just strolling around and seen you. We always hit up ones we never seen before. What's your name?"

"Isaac," he said.

I paused for a minute and remembered I had to head home to help my moms out. I told the kid I'd be back soon if he wanted me to.

"Yeah bro, that's cool just pull up anytime you feel like coming," Isaac said with no problem.

The next day I decided to go hit him up and chill for a bit. I pull up to his crib and he isn't there, I continue walking around the block and just wander somewhere else. I approach a large crew of cats I knew I wasn't coo with, then a familiar face was exposing out in the middle, wearing an ironed black tee, shorts with long white socks, and the same pearled white shoes he had on yesterday.

"You kickin it with these lames?" I approached and asked Isaac.

As I asked the question the group got triggered. I knew they would have but fuck it. One of the tallest cats made a remark, "Whats up, got a problem?" wearing an ironed navy shirt, creased khakis, and black kicks. I looked him up and down, and just made a smirk. He isn't worth my time, neither of them are.
Isaac finally spoke and answered the question, "Yeah, just met em' last night."

"Damn, all bad. That's on you though homeboy. Cant fuck with you if you're going to be rockin' with these fools, I'll see you around."

I walked off and never spoke to Isaac again, he became apart of the crew with the cats I ran into trouble with. I stood on my own and continued to do what I had to do.

Part Five
HORIZONS

God's Ears Are Never Open When I Speak
By Alondra Padilla

"I talk to god but the sky is empty" I disagree with this quote. The reason why I disagree is because I believe that god is real and I also believe that god listens to you when you talk to him. I believe that because I was raised in a Christian home. My parents have always been religious. I didn't believe in God I always argued with my parents that God wasn't real and that he didn't listen. I always thought the worst about God. I thought that he wouldn't ever listen to what people told him. I always thought that people who prayed just made themselves look because I thought it was just a huge waste of time. But now it's completely different and I'll tell you why.

I remember that on July 9, I prayed to god in the walls of a hospital. I had one of my family members really sick. I remember I was so scared and worried that something bad would happen to her and i knew I wouldn't be able to deal with the pain mainly seeing my dad fall into depression when he had a whole church to carry on his back. Every morning and the first thing I would do was pray. I remember praying before going to sleep. I did it for a whole week. I felt a good feeling after I prayed. I felt relax and I felt like everything was in control and that nothing bad would happen to my grandma.

My father got the news that his mom was better that she was now out of comma and she would be able to move and talk to us. As soon as I heard that i remembered all the times i prayed and talked to god. I still don't call myself a true Christian. I believe that god does not have a religion. I believe that god loves everyone the same and sees everyone the same way. I believe that god listens to your prayers. The skies are opened and God can hear. It's crazy to think that hospital walls have more prayers than church walls.

Identity Essay
By Bibi

I always felt quite normal, like there wasn't much difference between myself and others. I mean what really is different? We all have noses, ears, lips, hands. Though, yes there is in fact differences, like we all are a different age have different amount of siblings, live life differently, have different opinions basically, have a different way of thinking. Although it's not like I really kept that in mind while being 10 years old.

Though Las Vegas is my home I didn't always live here. Actually, thinking about it getting used to a new environment wasn't hard, and in the United States! I was all for it. Too young to not understand as much, but old enough to understand that well coming here was a pretty big fucking deal.

The United States has changed so much since Trump was elected. Definitely not for good, not for someone like me. There's moments I think about him and his power. People's opinions too on "people like me" and it's actually terrifying what they have to say, what he has to say.

Since when is a whole race defined by what one group of people choose to do or have to say. "Criminals." Sounds like major bullshit to me. Tell that to all those parents who came here with nothing just to give us everything. People just like Trump that came here to achieve more, to do more. Some even escaping the horror that they've experienced.

This experience showed me something about my identity that I didn't know about, like who knew? Maybe a lot of people, but me. I'm actually sad to know my way of being different.

There's nothing more horrific than knowing any morning might be my last with my parent, or a friend. Your average white girl will never have to worry about losing her family by having them be sent somewhere one day while you are at school.

In a way I'm left feeling like the place I consider home is just somewhere I happen to be trespassing at. I noticed some difference when I visited Utah and Caliente. Much of people there look a lot lighter than me, which was always interesting to me. But I never really mind it, now I just wonder if they do.

In a way I understand that I am in fact from somewhere else, but nobody should ever feel like they have to hide in order to want to be somewhere, especially their home. I'm sad that this is the realization I had with my identity, but at the end of the day I'll always be glad to be where I'm from and also be grateful to live here, it all has so much to do with my identity so why think any less about it.

Youngjae
By Marisol Diaz Nunez

The night was cold, as I walked through the streets of Seoul on my way home. I pulled at my red scarf slightly, to see if I could feel some warmth in this cold. As I crossed the street, I saw an old homeless man with only a small thick jacket freezing on the sidewalk. I watched for a while as people ignored him. I walked over to him removing, what was my favorite scarf, placing it on the man. He looked up in confusion but his eyes filled with gratitude.

"Thank you so much, young man you are too kind," he thanked, I smiled knowing that he won't be so cold anymore. I waved him goodbye but not before giving him some money to buy some food.

I began my walk back to the house, I walked a few steps passed the familiar convention store. I thought for awhile when I decided to walk in to get some snack for Jimin, and Min. I wondered a bit, letting my eyes adjust to the bright lights of the store, while looking for snacks I know Jimin, and Min would want. Hearing the faint buzzing within the store I found myself near the chip aisle. I held both the barbecue flavored chips and the lemon one, in my hands along with two strawberry flavored sodas.

When I walked to the register to pay, I noticed a lady with her two kids paying for instant meal packs. One of the little kids waved at me, in return I offered a smile, that he gladly returned. As I looked back at the mother, I noticed she was a few dollars short, without hesitation I pulled out the needed amount and held my hand out to the other older little boy next to her. He hesitated before I gave him a nod of assurance to take it. He placed the few dollars on the counter, his mother looked at him surprised before looking back at me, confirming I was the one that gave him the money. I could only offer her a smile that told her it was okay, with that she gave me a small bow of gratitude with I returned in respect to her.

I walked up for my chance to pay. When the familiar worker asked.

"You're too sweet, you know that?", my eyes widened slightly before scoffing at his comment.

"I'm not sweet, I just like helping others," I mused a small smirk noticeable on my lips.

"Being too nice has made you trust to many wrong people, Youngjae," he commented, with that said I sighed knowing he was right.

"I know, but what else can I do, Hyunjin?" I questioned, he smiled before he gave a somewhat serious expression.

"For starters, you can go on a date with me," he offered I let out a small laugh knowing he somewhat meant what he said. The amount of times, I was either dating or unhappy, he still asks me the same question. Just like the first time we met. But I've had my answer ready for when he asks. After we finished sharing a small laugh fit, I looked him with the equal amount of seriousness he had.

"Let me take you up on that offer," I smiled as his reaction grew to a very excited look.

"How about we watch a movie, and I'll take you to dinner, does friday work for you?" he coaxed, I thought if I had any plans which then made me realize I don't go out often enough to even have plans.

"Friday works perfect, you have my number so just tell me what time to get ready by and I'll be ready," I assured our plans as he handed my bag of items. I walked to the exit ready to leave as I waved goodbye he waved back, but not before blowing his signature flying kiss at me which I always laughed at. Know with my purchase done, I yawned as I reached the familiar apartment complex, putting in my code while grabbing my keys ready to open the door, just then it flew opened. I saw both Min and Jimin with half relieved and worried expressions written on their faces.

"You could at least messaged us you're gonna be a little late," chided Min as she pulled me into the warm environment we called home.

"Your brother is too forgetful," Jimin laughed which caused Min to lightly hit his shoulder in annoyance.

"I'm sorry sis, I promise I'll try to let you know beforehand next time," I assured her, she nodded in response.

"Alright then, anyways dinner is on the table, hope you like it" she chirped, before I walked over away from their point of view, I decide to drop the news.

"Oh yeah, I'm going on a date tomorrow with Hyunjin," I announced, as I sat down on the table taking in a whiff of the smell of, Bulgogi, one of my favorite dishes. As I took a big bite I heard both Min and Jimin scream out in shock.

"FINALLY!" All I could do was laugh at their reactions which I was anticipating. I continued eating thinking about what to wear tomorrow for my date.

"I hope it goes well," I smiled.

Rhyme Poem
By Kylie Cazares

Figuring out that I was nothing
Later on realizing that I was something.
Living life to the fullest.
Creating my own story
Sailing the seas showing off my glory.
I may be a small speck of dust when you're further away.
Yes it might be true
But once you see something that might be true to you.
You'll see the world in a whole other perspective.
And once you see the way i see it.
Life will lead you in a whole other direction.
I know that most of us just feel like we want to quit.
But,
Don't be that person who's always complaining
And grunting.
Remember, it's either all or nothing.
And once you're older you'll realize it too.
You'll think of that one thing in life that you never thought you knew.

El Principe
By Angel Obeso-Ferracin

I was at the racetrack. I could smell the wet dirt and the horse manure. The horse's coats shone in the bright summer sunlight, and the skittish horse's hooves lifted and fell in nervousness. My horse was in the 2nd stall and was getting ready to race. 300 yards was the distance, and I wasn't sure if I was more nervous or he was... We had trained him all year and this was his big moment. As he got in the barrier my heart started beating faster.

And there in and count to 10 began... As he came out the starting barrier it jump out in front. Good race so far, they were coming fast. At around 100 yards it was a tight race, they were very close with each other running. As I recorded the race I was so nervous, my hands got sweaty, then my phone started slipping out of my hands. Luckily I caught grip and was able to sustain my phone to keep recording. As they were coming my horse and the other one were coming side by side, such a tight race it was for either.

By about 250 yards the other horse took a slight lead. Losing by about the full head of the other horse my horse started running harder as the finish line was near. At that moment my heart was beating so fast and hard I thought I was going to get a heart attack. As soon as they passed the 300 yard finish line I stopped recording and replayed the race on my phone. I put it in slow motion and paused it right at the finish line but I wasn't sure. The race was so close I couldn't tell if we had won. I was very nervous waiting for the officials to announce the winners... After what had felt like forever the officials finally were about to announce the winner...

And the winner of this years derby is 'El Principe' from stall #2. I was so happy I started jumping up and down cheering. I remember running to my dad and jumping to give him a hug. We were so happy, it was a big accomplishment... but then that happiness was ripped away from us... As we looked over we saw our horse on the ground and we started running to him. As we got there I saw how he was trying to make an effort to get up, but he couldn't. We started to help him up and as he got up I thought everything was going to be okay. But about 4 steps was all he walked then he collapsed... I then felt sad and all the happiness was gone. As I watched my horse die my eyes got watery. That day although we won a good, hard race, it wasn't the same because our winner was gone.

He left a lot of good memories and will never be forgotten...

Something I learned about myself is that I am very close to horses and I have a lot of love for them. Another thing I learned was that appreciate the people you care about. And although a horse is an animal and not a person you have to treat it the same, with lots of love and care.

Valentine
By Noah Baldridge

As I throw the already-wilted bouquet of flowers away, a dinky old lady pauses and looks at me. "Those must be the most beautiful flowers i've ever seen!" she exclaims. "They were for a beautiful woman," I reply and hand them to her instead. As I further my lonesome way home I stop and give a heart-shaped box of chocolates to a scraggly homeless man. He thanks me and tells me they are the best chocolates he's ever had. As I continue home I come across a small boy with a backpack and a puzzled look on his face. "What wrong bud? Where's your mommy?" As I suspected he replies with I don't know and small, frightened tears. I hand him a teddy bear that is holding a heart that reads "Be mine" and tell him to calm down, and with a healthy face full of the teddy bear he stops. He reckalects the past events and within no time he's content in the worriefull warm embrace of his mother. She thanks me one thousand and one times and all I offer is a "Glad I could be here."

What My Parents Expected
By Jaquelyn Martinez

I am a 15 year old latina girl living in the 21st century, where latina girls are known to have bodies with curves. Where latina girls aren't the brightest people. And where latina women are seen as just housewives. See I come from a household where the women has to do all the house chores such as cooking, cleaning, taking care of the kids etc. And the man of the house is the one going to work everyday to earn the money needed to maintain their families. Ever since I was a little girl I was always taught how to wash the dishes properly, how to fold the sheets, how to put in loads of laundry, how to sweep, etc. I remember wanting to play with dinosaurs or nerf guns as a kid, but my dad would always tell me " no mija, those aren't things you can play with" or he'd say " mija don't get all dirty in the mud you need to look nice for when company gets here". I would sit there and look at him upset because I realized I wasn't allowed to be like a guy. I had to learn how to have manners sooner than my brothers I had to learn how to clean so I could clean my brothers rooms. And as I got older and made more latina girlfriends I came to realize that our parents taught us that we are "wanted" by a guy due to our ability of being "wifey" material. But as I got older I stopped doing my parents chores for their reasonings and started doing those same chores for my own reasons. I realized that them giving me those type of responsibilities wasn't going to help me get the guy in my life that I needed. But I realized that they were going to teach me how to be an independent women at a young age. My parents may have not liked that idea but it didn't matter. I wasn't going to be that girl that did things because she needed a man to depend on. I am going to be that girl that does things so I don't have to depend on any man to help me maintain myself. I used my parents "expectations" for myself.

Say It Before It's Too Late
By Jaquelyn Martinez

We never know when the last time we're going to see a person will be. It could be today, tomorrow, two weeks from now, or even two weeks ago. Now I'm not saying it'll be due to life taking its course. No, many people just lose contact, stop talking due to disagreements/issues, or don't talk until "next time". But the truth is you don't know if there will be a next time do you?

You hang out with your friends and family thinking about the next time you'll see them and think to yourself "oh, next time I see them I'll tell them about this". Or you hang out with your crush and you tell yourself "okay, next time I talk to him/her I'll tell them how I feel". But the thing is by next time, you might forget what you were going to tell them, or you'll be too scared to tell your crush that you like them. I know this from experience.

Just a few weeks ago my uncle was arrested for a DUI. I'm not gonna lie we used to get in many arguments because of him being an alcoholic,and due to a lot of that arguing I never really told him how much I loved him. But he had just been arrested and put in jail so I could still go and visit him, but never did because I was so angry with him. Till one morning my dad gets a phone call, "ICE got your uncle mija" is all I hear. I ran upstairs to my room and cried for hours. I regret not spending more time with him for fun rather than bickering at him, but I mostly regret never telling my uncle that I loved him in person.

Don't waste your time being too afraid to tell someone how you really feel. Tell them before it's too late. Don't wait till next time and don't wait until you're confident enough to do it because you don't know if there is a next time. You might think about next time but you never know what can happen. So do yourself a favor, man up and let your feelings out, it's okay to be vulnerable at times, it's okay to tell people that you're angry, but it's not okay to hold it in and regret it because you never got to tell that person what they mean to you.

I Believe That People Should Not Be Homophobic
By Nereida Delgado

I believe that people is so dumb for being a homophobic just because they said that is bad or a sin. I mean that there is nothing bad being part of the LGBT community, or if it is bad they can explain to me why it is bad or why "I'm going to hell". Being lesbian, gay, bisexual, etc. I think is something that is not just words that someone say just because they want to say it. When someone say that is part of the LGBT community is because is something that they feel and like. For example me, I'm bisexual/lesbian my family tell me that they never gonna accept me because doesn't accept it.

When family tell me that I was so sad because there is nothing bad with that and I'm normal like them. I just like something different. They criticize without knowing 100% because it is bad. They only rely on things they see in the bible but they do not know about them. But aya they not accept me when I grow up I will do with my life what I want because I will be of age and can not stop me in my decisions.

I would feel a very privileged person if my family accepts me as I am but then I can not. I admire and I envy people who come out and their families accept them. I think that the people who accept them as they are are one of the most lucky people in the world. Parents and families who accept their children who are LGBT are some of the people who fail to value because I feel they are very wise and smart to care about the happiness of the people they love. But we do not all have these people and we have to learn to live with that, however it may be.

I think that is why many times for these reasons many young people commit suicide. I think the most important thing for a person who likes someone of the same sex is that their families accept them. The family is the most important thing there and one feels more sure of themselves, if they had that great support. As for example in school I am someone but in my house, that is so trite because you can not be who you really want to be for fear of being criticized. But I know that the day will come when I will be happy because I know my goals will come.

The Curly Headed Girl
By Emely Alarcon

When I first went into kindergarten I immediately noticed that I was one of the only ones in my classroom that had curly hair, my mom didn't really know what to do with my hair so every morning my mom would give me a slick back ponytail with a thick layer of hairspray so not even one little curl would stick out. And I didn't really know that I would hate my hair so much until I would see all theses girls with straight hair and there fingers can just glide straight through it and not get in a billion nots like mine. The first time I straightened my hair was in the 7th grade and it wasn't even straightened good, you could still see the waves in the root of my hair there was still some little curly babie hairs sticking out it was just all bad. My parents would get so mad at me when I straightened my hair they would say "porque te estas camando tu pello esta tan bonito" But I knew they were only telling me that because I was there daughter and they were obligated to say that. I despised my dad just a little bit for giving me the gene of curly hair i just wanted to have straight hair like my mom, and not have the problem of waking up with that crazy hair it was like it was crazy hair day for me every morning. At least didn't have to do anything on crazy hair day that's one perk.

And I would spend hours watching youtube videos on how to straighten my hair. Which seemed simple you just run the straightener through your hair but it was much more than that. You had I have this serum and you have to have heat protecting spray and all these things just so your hair wouldn't get damaged. And it was just too much just to straighten your hair and it's not worth it.

And I just to lazy to do all of that and actually take an hour of my day sitting and straightening my hair. So I just didn't do anymore and the more I stopped doing it the more I started to like my hair, I was like wow I actually don't hate something about myself. And i started searching ways to style my hair so it won't like I just woke up and head out the door. And I started to feel more confident and showed my hair off more. No more tight ponytails that would look like you got botoxs on your face and give you a huge headache of how tight they were. And I also didn't have to spend hours curling my hair because my hair was already curly. I also realized that curly hair has some perks it like not having to curl your hair. And it adds some characteristics to me because to me like without my curly hair I wouldn't feel like myself.

I learned how to style my hair so it wouldn't look so messy and frizzy and I started taking care of it more I did so much research on how to make it even more curly which was something that I avoided to do for a long time. I never wanted my hair to be more curly than what it was that was my worst nightmare before. And I realized that there were more positives to my hair then there was negatives.

I finally accepted that my hair is a part of me and that I shouldn't hate it because it's different from what other people have. And I started to notice that once I felt more confident in my hair I started to feel better about myself. And I also notice that a lot of latinas had curly hair and I am latina. So my curly hair is not also part of my identity it's also a part of my ethnicity and my culture and I was even more proud to have my curly hair.

This I Believe... About Love
By Kylie Cazares

A psychology study suggests that when you're single, all you see are happy couples. When you're committed or in a relationship, you see happy singles. When I think about it now, most of the time, this is true. I notice the couple that holds hands while walking to their destination. I see those couples that sit on a bench leaning against each other. I see those couples that give each other a hug before one enters their class. But does it have to matter to me?

Does that mean that I miss holding that person's hand? Or putting my head against their shoulder? Or giving them that goodbye hug before I enter the classroom? No. It doesn't have to mean anything like that. You might just miss that person, or having the feeling of wanting to be loved, isn't what most people want these days? They just enter a relationship because they feel lonely, because they want to feel loved by someone.

Not for me. Most of the people I know want someone to love in their life. And right then and there, they've already made a mistake. People ask me if I'm interested in someone once in awhile and I always reply with the same answer, "No." When I say this in a truthful way, they either stare at me in disbelief or state that I'm lying.

Most of the time I'm honest because I haven't met a person who I would think would be right for me. I believe that I shouldn't just suddenly like someone just because of the way they look or do the things that interest me. I think that I should get to know someone first, to see what type of person they are, what they do for fun, what they believe in. I believe that I have to feel a connection between us.

One of my friends one day just starts complaining about all of the couples she sees and why she couldn't find someone for her. The next day she comes up to me and says that she started having feelings for an old friend at our school. I asked her why she suddenly started liking him. She replied with these words that said it all, "I don't know, he just seems like a nice guy and I've known him for a while." I didn't even have to see her actions, her words told me everything. She had already made a mistake.

It takes the typical person 17 months and 26 days to get over an ex. Another psychological study. I've realized that in the past when I started dating someone, I would usually look around to find my ex and try to see if he saw my new partner and I together holding hands. The more time that had past, the more I realized why I started dating the guy. I was just trying to make that someone else jealous. I've been making a mistake.

Infatuation is when you find somebody who is absolutely perfect, love is when you realize that they aren't and it doesn't matter. I found someone back then who, I believe, was someone who would change my life forever. There were those times when he would bring out the weird side of him, I didn't question it because I didn't care. I only cared about what I felt about him, not what I thought. And somehow, I was still making a mistake even when I thought I was doing what I believe.

I feel like these days most people just get into a relationship just because they don't want to be single anymore, not all of them, but most. My only reason for liking someone is because I feel like we have that bond that can be hard to break. I don't like them just because I've been single for a "long period of time" and "need to move on." I believe that people should get into a relationship for the bond that they share together and the things that make them feel that bond. I can't explain what I'm really trying to say just in words, but I think you get the idea.

Sato and Veronica
By Carlos Ordaz

"Ha..looked at your face now you dumbass,that's what you get for messing with us!?"

But they didn't know that I actually lost on purpose so it wouldn't get suspicious because I didn't want my anger to cause another accident.

On the way home I was thinking why they would fight me to get attention to show power. That's the most dumbest reason to fight one person. Even I wouldn't fight someone for that but I could've at least show some of my power but it still would've been suspicious but oh well.

After that situation the next day rumors spread about what happened but it still wouldn't faze me because they are mere peasants to my plan. But I would still need to keep this act of being the silent guy in the back but it irritates me too much cause of the annoyance of these people. But there was one girl that actually cared to what happened to me.

"Hey Sato what happened to you?" said Veronica.

"Oh hey Veronica, nothing happened" said Sato.

"You sure I heard rumors that you got into a fight with John" said Veronica.

"Yeah don't worry, it's alright" said Sato.

One week later John tried to start another fight with Sato but Sato couldn't hold his anger and let it all out onto John and his little group. But later got arrested for brutally beating John and his group. Now 4 months later on his release date Veronica came to see him and took him to his apartment that he live by himself.

"Hey I'm glad that you're alright" said Veronica.

"Yeah it was alright inside there" said Sato.

"So your gonna go back to school now or what" said Veronica.

"No I don't think that going to school would be the best option right now, I might find me a job at the moment and I'll think of the rest" said Sato.

"Alright but I'll come and visit you time by time" said Veronica.

"Alright I'll be okay with you visiting me" said Sato.

After that they both grew up with each other and later became a couple to live happily till they would get old.

AUTHOR BIOGRAPHIES

Emely Alarcon is a 15 year old with a creative and outstanding attitude. That attitude can turn something little into something big for the better or the worse.

Elivs Arias I am a student at equipo academy school east las vegas, and I like playing with my nephew and love to be with my family, I love dogs and they are fun to play with them. i thought life was easy but actually it i hard.

Esmeralda Arroyo is a sophomore at Equipo Academy who aspires to be the best writer she can be.

Steve Arroyo Jr., out here in the field doing the most, no destruction but reckless, humble. From the East of LA to the 702. StonerWays.

Arturo Barraza is a young 15yrs old Mexican who stays in these streets tryng to change his ways. From East LV.

Kylie Cazares is a sophomore who aspires to explore the world and discover new things. She writes about the life she pictures for herself in the future in stories of other characters.

Marisol Diaz Nunez is a 16-year-old sophomore and a big Kpop fan. She has a loving family whom inspire her everyday. Her mind is always wondering and thinking of new ideas. She doesn't consider herself the best but she is happy to share her proud work with the world.

Michael Elena, a terrific scholar taking big risks, no mater the struggle or circumstances keep on pushing and a big hustler!

Abraham Esqueda is a 15 year old know at all cocky 10th grade scholar. He brags about his talents in a way where he doesn´t so that others can say otherwise. Doesn´t like to talk at times, yet quite enough to have a big voice. Overall, this guy has a great and specialized personality.

Angel Ferracin is a 10th grader that goes to Equipo Academy. He loves food and money.

David Henry is an inspiring poet who attends Equipo Academy in Las Vegas, Nevada. He is fifteen years old and originally from Los Angeles, California. He is best known for his unique and touching poetry.

Kevin Hernandez I am a student at equipo academy in east las vegas We all have two lives. The second one starts when we realize we only have one i realized that wen i came to this school i thought life was easy and all that but in reality its more to that story life is all about risks

Bryan Herrera 16-year-old male who enjoys playing soccer.

Carlos Lainez is a young scholar who is currently attending Equipo Academy. He is a hard working student, who tries his best at everything.

Carlos Martinez is a 17-year-old male athlete. He is a student at Equipo Academy.

Jaquelyn Martinez is a sophomore at Equipo Academy that likes to write about anything that comes to mind.

Marizela Montalvo is a 16 year old student at Equipo Academy working to achieve her goals and intending on making her family and friends proud.

Miguel Oliva is a young intellectual 16 year old that is attending Equipo Academy. He is a hardworking positive young adolescent with a bright future Who loves his friends and family.

Carlos Ordaz is a 16-year-old sophomore at Equipo Academy. He enjoys playing soccer and enjoys writing deep poetry.

Alondra Padilla is a 16-year-old student athlete who goes to Equipo Academy. Reading and writing has changed her life completely and she didn´t consider herself a writer until now.

Andrea Padilla is a sophomore student at Equipo Academy. She loves her puppies.

Diego Padilla a hardworking 10th grader that goes to Equipo Academy that is a successful writer and the original creator of John Marston.

Maximus Pineda is a sophomore at Equipo Academy. He is an inspiring artist. He enjoys TV, music, art and video games. Maximus hopes to become an animator, story board artist,concept artist, and video game developer.

Alejandro Renteria a young singer that wants to prosper and take his family out the poor.

Jacob Sellers is a student at Equipo Academy who likes to work hard to get the best grades he can.

Made in the USA
Coppell, TX
11 December 2024